Google Classroom

Easiest Teacher's Guide to Master Google Classroom

Teacher's Guide Table of Contents

Student's Guide Table of Contents

Introduction

Congratulations on downloading *Google Classroom* and thank you for doing so.

Are you a teacher that wants to make your class more organized and effective?

That is what Google Classrooms is going to do!

Classrooms are going to make it to where you are no longer have to give out papers to your class and you are going to be able to monitor the progress of your students as they fulfill the requirements for that class.

Google Classrooms is going to make it to where you are able to save time and make your class run more efficiently as well as make sure that your students are able to do what needs to be done.

Google Classrooms is going to change the way that education is delivered to students and ultimately change education around the world!

The following chapters will discuss how Google is making it to where teachers are going to be able to reach out to students in numerous ways. Google classroom is going to be a way that teachers, students, and parents are all going to be on the same page and it is less likely that a student will lose his homework.

You are going to see that using Google Classroom is going to make it to where as a teacher, you are not going to have to deal with a lot of the headaches that you deal with when having to print out all the assignments that your students need thanks to the fact that it is all online!

There are plenty of books on this subject on the market, thanks again for choosing this one! Every effort was made to ensure it is full of as much useful information as possible, please enjoy!

Chapter one: What is Google Classroom?

The point behind Google Classroom is to offer a platform of blended learning in schools in order to simplify creating assignments and getting the grade out to the students in a paperless way.

Google Classroom was first introduced as something that could be added to G Suite for Education back in 2014 when it was first created and it was released to the public August of that year. June of the following year, it was announced that Google Classroom would have a share button that would enable administrators and developers to continue to engage with Google Classroom.

March of 2017 brought the classroom being opened for personal use for Google users so that they could join classes without needing an education account. April also made it possible for Google users on personal accounts to be able to create and teach classes as they see fit.

Google Classroom took Google Drive and added it to the classroom so that assignments could be created and sent out to the students. Google docs and slides and sheets are used for writing and Gmail is used for communicating back and forth. Finally, the calendar is going to be used to schedule assignments so that students can see what is coming up without having to write it down and lose the paper that they used to write it down on.

Students are going to be invited to classes through the database that is created by the school by using a private code or by being imported through the school's domain. Every class that is made will have a folder that is going to have its own path to that classes drive where students can turn their work in to be graded.

Teachers are going to be able to monitor each student's progress and return work after it has been graded. The teacher can comment on homework so that the students know what they did wrong so that they can improve. Teachers are also going to be able to create class announcements which students will have the ability to comment on.

Google has made claims that Google classroom is not going to show ads if used as part of G Suite for Education due to the fact it is not going to be collecting data for advertising purposes.

Chapter two: Google Classroom Assignments

Any assignment that is created for Google Classroom is going to be stored and graded on the productivity applications that Google offers so that the teacher and student or a group of students can work together.

Rather than sharing documents that are on the Google Drive of the student, the files are going to be hosted by the drive of the student and then submitted to the teacher for grading. A teacher is going to have the option of choosing a file to use as a template in order to allow the students to copy it and make it their own before turning it in rather than the students being allowed to copy or edit the exact same document.

Students are also going to be able to choose if they want to add extra documents to their drive for that particular assignment or not.

Chapter three: Google Classroom Grading

There are several different grading schemes that you are going to be able to choose from as the teacher. You can either attach files for the assignments that the students need to complete so the entire class has access to that attachment. Or, each student can get an individual copy of the assignment.

A student will take files and create them so that they can attach them to the assignment in the event that the teacher did not give them a copy that they could use for their assignment.

As the teacher, you are going to have the ability to monitor the progress that every student is making on their assignment as well as having the option to make comments and edit their assignments.

The assignments that are turned in and graded will be sent back to the student with comments from the teacher so that things can be revised and turned back in done correctly. After the assignment is completely graded, the assignment can only be edited by the teacher unless the teacher sends the document back to the student.

Chapter four: Communicating with Google Classroom

Teachers are going to have the option of posting announcements in a class stream which will then be able to be commented on by the students so that the student and the teacher can communicate about any questions that may arise for that particular assignment.

A student is going to have the option of posting in the class stream but it is not going to be made high priority by Google Classroom because it is not posted by the teacher. Various media types can be used for announcements such as videos from YouTube or files that are located in Google Drive.

Gmail is also going to give teachers and students the option to communicate inside of the interface for Google Classroom.

Students and teachers alike are going to have the ability to access their classroom on the computer or through applications that are made available on mobile devices that use iOS or Android operating systems.

Chapter five: The Time Cost of Using Google Classroom

In order to add a student to a class, the students are going to be given a code from their teacher that is going to get them into the private group specific for that class. The teacher is going to manage several different classes and will be able to reuse the announcements, questions, and assignments that they have used in other classes.

Posts can also be shared across multiple classes and even saved so that they can be used for future classes.

The work, questions, grades, comments, and anything else that is placed in the classroom is going to be sorted so that the teacher will know what is needing to be reviewed. Therefore, saving paper and the teacher is not going to be searching for lost assignments or looking for what they are needed to deal with at that moment.

Chapter six: Archiving Courses

As the class instructor, you are going to be able to archive the course whenever the semester or year ends that way you can use it for a different year.

After a class has been archived, it is going to be taken down from the homepage and moved into the folder where the archived classes are going to be so that the teacher is able to continue to keep that class organized.

Students and teachers are still going to be able to view what is inside of an archived class, however they are not going to be able to modify anything until it has been restored.

Chapter seven: Mobile Applications for Google Classroom

There are mobile applications for Google Classroom that were first introduced in January of 2015. You are going to be able to download these applications on any device that uses iOS or Android operating systems.

These apps make it possible for students and teachers to take photos and turn them in with the assignment as well as share files that are located in other applications and even make it to where you can access the classroom offline if needed.

Chapter eight: The Privacy of Google Classrooms

Google Classrooms are going to have different privacy than other Google services. Since Google Classroom is part of the Education suite that is offered by Google, there are not going to be any advertisements that are shown.

Whenever in the interface, the students and other staff are not going to get their data scanned or used for any advertising purposes.

In fact, data is not going to be collected off of anything from Google Classrooms in order to protect the privacy of the school and its students and staff.

Chapter nine: The Reception of Google Classrooms

The eLearningIndustry made a review of Google Classroom after they tested it. In their review, they highlighted that there are both positive and negative aspects to Google Classroom.

One of the strengths that Google Classroom has is that it is easy to use, uses Google Drive in an effective way that makes it easy for teachers to share assignments, it is accessible on almost any device, and it is paperless. Another advantage is that it offers immediate feedback from the teacher to the students.

Some of the disadvantages are that there is a heavy integration process with the Google apps and service that are limited and do not have any support to go with them when it comes to external files or services. There is the lack of automated quizzes and tests, no discussion forms or live chats that can be used for feedback and helping students with their assignments.

Google is always being criticized for allegedly data mining the history and searches from students accounts in order to use it for advertising purposes. However, in April of 2014, it was announced that the emails of students would no longer be scanned in order to fix the privacy concerns of parents and other Google members.

It was written by TechCrunch that the ads are not included in the educational program data and information that is pulled from their users.

Chapter ten: Your Google Classroom

It is only going to take a few minutes to create a new class or post resources or even set permissions for your students. After you have done this you are going to be able to invite students directly to the class or by sending them a code.

Creating classes

1. On a computer, you are going to go to classroom.Google.com
2. Select the plus sign then choose the create class button.
3. You will then enter the name of the class.
4. Enter in text like grade level and what time the class is.
5. Also put a subject line in
6. Select create.

Your class is going to automatically be given a code that is going to be used to invite students. You have the option of changing the themes and putting a photo for the class. Should you not need the class anymore you can archive it.

Accepting provisioned classes

Whoever manages the classroom is going to be able to create classes for their teachers as well as adding students to them. Any classes that are made by the administrator are going to be placed in a provisioned state. As the teacher you will need to sign in and accept the invitation to the class before it is visible to students.

1. Go to classroom.Google.com
2. Move to the classes card and choose accept.
3. Ensure that the number of students in the class is accurate before choosing accept.

Changing the theme

Once you have created the class, you have the option of changing the image and colors of the class. Only teachers have the ability to change the theme.

1. Sign into classroom.Google.com
2. Move to the bottom of the class image and choose the select theme button.
3. Pick one of the following options
   a. Pick a pattern.
   b. Choose an image from the gallery.

Uploading your own image

1. Open your class and pick upload photo.
2. Pick one of these options
   a. Move a picture over to the middle of the screen.
   b. Select a photo from your computer.

Editing class information

1. Enter classroom.Google.com into your URL
2. Move to the class card and select the three little dots. A menu will pop up which will give you the option of editing the class.
3. Enter the new information and hit save.

Displaying a profile picture

You have the ability to place a photo next to the name of your class. Automatically your classroom is going to use your Google account photo so you will want to make sure that you are using an appropriate picture.

Problems creating classes

In the event that you are using a G Suite Education account and find that you are unable to add classes, then the administrator of the suite is going to need to verify that you are a teacher in their domain. So, make sure that you are contacting your administrator for any help that you may need.

Note: should you be using a personal Google account, then you are going to be limited on how many classes you are going to be able to create.

Adding a class to a resource page

Once a class has been created, you are going to have the ability to add class information and resources to your class in the about page. You are going to be able to post materials and instructions for your class so that they can know how you grade, what to expect throughout the year, so on so forth. This information can be added or removed at any point in time.

Adding class information

1. Go to the website classroom.Google.com
2. Move to the about section. The name of the class is going to automatically be entered there.
3. You can add in a description or a location for the class. But, if you leave these fields blank, they are not going to appear in what the students see for your class.
4. Save.

Resource materials

1. Under the class information section you will see a button that says add class materials and a title can be entered there.
2. You will have the option of adding in multiple resources under one title or adding them in separately under specific names.
   a. In order to attach a file, click on the appropriate icon.
   b. Find the item that you are wanting to attach and click add. Should you decide that you do not need that item anymore just click on remove.
   c. Post.

Your email address and a link to the folder where the attachment is located will be automatically included with every item that is added to the resource page. This cannot be changed.

Editing your about page

1. Go to the classroom web page.
2. Move to the about section.
3. Click on the three dots and select the edit button.
4. Make any changes that you see fit and then save them.

Joining classes by invitation

You can not only create your own class, but you can be invited to classes so that you can become a co teacher in a class. Co teachers are going to have the option of performing all of the teacher tasks once they have joined that class.

Accepting an invitation

1. Go to the classroom web page.
2. Accept the invitation or decline it if you do not want to be a co teacher.
3. You can also select the invitation through the email that you get.

Note: when a student declines the invitation to become a co teacher, they are not going to be removed from the class.

Inviting teachers to a class

Teachers can be invited to co teach a class or to help coordinate class activities. In using Google groups, groups of teachers can be invited at the same time.

Inviting co teachers or groups of co teachers

You are not going to have to be the owner of the group but you are going to need to be a member of the group in order to be invited others to the group.

1. Log into your classroom.
2. Go to the class that you are wanting to add co teachers to.
3. Move to the about section.
4. Click on the invite teachers button.
5. Individual teachers or groups of teachers can be entered by entering the group email or the teacher's email.
6. Click on the teacher or group and select add.
7. You can invite as many teachers or groups as you want by repeating the same steps.
8. Select invite.

Note: your class is going to be updated to show those who have been invited. An email is going to be received by the teacher so that they can join the class by clicking on the join class card.

Permissions for co teachers

These permissions are going to need to be made aware of by all of the teachers in a class.

- Only the main teacher has the ability to delete the class.
- Co teachers who join a class can access the Google Drive folder.
- Primary teachers cannot withdraw or be removed from their own class.
- Teachers cannot be muted.
- The primary teacher is the owner of the Google Drive folder.

Class size

G Suite accounts

If you are using a G suite account then you are going to be able to have up to twenty teachers and a thousand members of both teachers and students

Note: Classrooms are going to use groups for the students and teachers that are using the education suite accounts. Every person is only going to be allowed in a certain number of groups.

Personal accounts

When using a personal account there are going to be other limits put on activities such as creating or inviting people.

Inviting students

Students are going to have to be enrolled in your class through an invitation or a code that is given to them by you. If you are using Google groups you can invite an entire group of students at the same time.

Inviting students or groups of students

You are not going to have to own the group to invite students, you just have to be a member of it.

1. Go to the classroom website.
2. Go to the class you are wanting to invite people to.
3. Move to students and then click on invite students.
4. You are going to be able to invite individual students or groups of students by entering their email address.
5. When looking at the search results, you are going to click on the student or the group of students before hitting add.
6. Invite more students by repeating steps four and five.
7. Select invite..

Note: the class will be updated once students select the join button on their class card

Giving out the class code

1. Log into your Google classroom.
2. Go to students and the code will be located to the left under class code.
3. Select copy.
4. Send the code to the students in an email or write it out on the board in your class whenever your students are setting up their accounts.

5. The students should follow these instructions
   a. Sign in to the classroom website.
   b. Go to join class on the home screen.
   c. Enter the code and then select join.

Inviting students not in the school domain

As long as the school administrator allows the permission to be turned on so that you can invite students to your class that are not in your school's domain

Resetting or disabling the class code

Should a student or students have a problem with your class code you can either reset it or disable it.

1. Go to your classroom.
2. Move to the students tab where the code is located.
3. Select the code and choose reset or disable.
4. If you want to enable a code that has been disabled just click on enable.

Removing a student

Whenever a student is taken out of a class their work is going to stay in their folder. You can delete their work and posts if you need to.

1. Go to Google Classrom.
2. Move to the student section.
3. Click on the box that appears next to the name of the student that needs to be removed.
4. Go to the top of the page and click on actions and then remove.
5. Make sure to hit confirm before removing the students.

Removing a teacher

The only person who can remove teachers from classes is the primary teacher. The primary teacher cannot be removed from their own class.

1. Log into Google Classrooms.
2. Go to the class that you are wanting to modify.
3. Go to the about section.
4. Locate the teacher's name and click on the three dots to open the menu.
5. Select remove from class.
6. Confirm and remove.

Archiving a class

When the semester or school year ends you have the option of archiving the class so you can use the material later. In archiving a class it is going to be removed so you no longer see it in an effort to keep your other classes organized.

Note: whenever a class becomes archived it will no longer show up on a students feed.

After a class has been archived it cannot be modified until it is restored.

1. Go to Google classroom
2. Move to the class card and select archive
3. Confirm to complete the process

Looking at an archived class

1. Go to your Google Classroom.
2. Select the menu and move to archived classes.

3. Select which class it is that you are wanting to look at.

Restoring an archived class

A class can be restored after it has been archived, all you are going to need to do is move to the class card so that you can update your class.

1. Log into Google Classroom.
2. Go to the archived classes menu.
3. Select the three dots and go to the restore option.
4. Click restore to confirm that you want the class to be restored.

Deleting a class that has been archived

When you permanently delete a class, it has to be archived first. Classes cannot be deleted unless they have been archived.

1. Move to the Google classroom website.
2. Select archived classes.
3. On the class card, click delete
4. Confirm your deletion.

Note: you cannot undo the deleting of a class. Once you have clicked the delete button you are not going to have access to that class any longer or anything that is going to be posted in it. The only thing that you will have access to is the files for that class that are located on the drive.

Tracking assignments and events

You will have the ability to track the questions and assignments that your class does on a calender. When a class is created in

Google Classroom, your students are going to see the class calender in your classroom as well as on their Google calender.

On the classroom calender, the students are going to see what assignments are due. On their Google calender, they will see the events that you add like test dates, field trips so on and so forth.

If there are no calenders see for your classes, then your administrator may have turned the calender permissions off for your account.

Viewing assignment due dates

Whenever an assignment is created, it will automatically add the due date to the class calender. Your students are going to be able tos ee these assignments in the classroom calender or their Google calender.

1. Log into Google Classroom.
2. Go to the menu located at the top of the page.
3. Select calender.
4. Pick an assignment or question and open it.
5. You can view past and future work by clicking the next button.
6. You can see the assignments for every class that you manage by selecting all classes. In order to see the assignments for a single class click on all classes and select which class you want to see.

Adding events to Google Calender

In order to track events like tests you will add them to your Google calender. All a student is going to have to do is open the calender and they will be able to see the events.

1. Go to Google classroom.
2. Select the class you want to view.
3. Go to the about section.
4. Next to the calender option, choose open in Google calender.

See posts and sharing permissions

Students are allowed to post messages in the class stream as well as comment on anything the teacher or their classmates may post. You are going to be able to control what the students post by setting up permissions for specific students or the entire class. You are also able to delete posts made by students.

Setting permissions for a class

1. Find the class that you are wanting to set the permissions for.
2. Go to the students section.
3. Choose a permission level from the post and comment list.
   a. Students are allowed to post and comment: this is going to be the default setting. Students are going to be able to share messages to the class stream and comment on anything that is posted in the class.
   b. Students can only comment: the students are not going to be allowed to share messages.
   c. Only teacher can post or comment: this is essentially muting all the students so that they cannot do anything but look at what you post.

Muting a student

When a student is muted, they are not going to be able to comment or post on the class stream. Other students are not going to see anything in the stream to show them that they have been muted. They are just not going to have the option of posting.

Muting students on the student page

1. Go to the class where the students are.
2. Go to the student tab.
3. Select the box next to the student that you want to mute.
4. Select actions and then mute.
5. Confirm the muting of the student.

Mute a student on their post or comment

1. Find the class where the student is.
2. Find where they have posted or commented.
3. Click on more and select mute "student's name".
4. Confirm the muting.
5. You can delete the comment by
   a. Clicking on the three dots and hitting delete
   b. Click on delete again

Unmuting a student

When unmuting a student, they are going to be able to post and comment on things in the class stream.

Unmute from the student page

1. Go to the students page.

2. Move to the students section.
3. Click on which students you want to unmute.
4. Go to actions and unmute.
5. Confirm and unmute once more.

Unmute from a post

1. Find the class the student is in.
2. Find where they have commented or messaged on something.
3. Click the three dots and select unmute "student name".
4. Confirm to unmute a student.

Delete a post or comment made by a student

1. Find the class you want to modify.
2. Find the post or comment and click on more.
3. Go to delete and then confirm.

Seeing what has been deleted

1. Go to the class where there are deleted comments or posts
2. Under the stream option click on show
3. In order to hide them, click hide and they will be hidden.

Chapter eleven: Gurdians and Google Classroom

If you are the guardian of a student who is using Google Classrooms, you are going to be able to receive summaries about your student that have school accounts.

These emails are going to give you a summary about the progress that your student is making in their class. You will have the option to choose how frequently you get the emails or you can unsubscribe from them at any time that you need to.

The guardian emails are going to include:

- Missing work: whenever work is late and has not been turned in.
- Upcoming work: work that is due that day or the next. This is only going to come on daily emails. If you are getting weekly emails, then you will get the work for that week.
- Class activity: anything that is posted by the teacher so that you can keep up making sure your student is doing their work.

Removing yourself as guardian

If at any point in time you want to remove yourself as the guardian of a student, you may do so. It is going to be easiest if you have a Google account.

1. Go to the bottom of an email summary and select settings
2. Find the students name and select the trashcan

However, if you do not have a Google account you will

1. Go an email summary and select unsubscribe.
2. You will have to click it again to make sure that you are aware you are permanently deleting yourself as guardian.

If you remove yourself as a guardian, the student is going to get an email allowing them to know.

Chapter twelve: Email Summaries

Email summaries are going to let you keep up to date about what is going on in your students class. Before you are able to get summaries, you need to first have a Google account due to the fact that it makes things a lot easier on you in the long run.

Creating a Google account

In order to manage your email summaries, you will need to get a free Google account. You are not going to need to have a Google email address to create the account, you are going to be able to use any email that you access most often.

1. Inside of the email program that you use, go to the bottom of an email summary and select the settings button.
2. When it goes to the email settings page, you will create a new account
3. From there you are going to fill out the information that is requested and submit it, then the email settings page is going to open.

Recieve email summaries

As the parent or guardian of a student, you are going to be enabled to recieve and accept an email invitation that is going to mean that you can recieve email summaries on your student. The only people who are going to be allowed to send out these invitations are the teachers or the administrators of the school.

Once the invitation has been sent, you are going to have a hundred and twenty days to accept the invitation or else it is going to expire.

1. The administrator or the teacher is going to send you an email invitation for a particular student. This email can be sent to any email that you want it sent to.
2. Once you get the invitation, you will go to the email and open it.
3. Next you will click accept. In the event that you are not the guardian of a student you are going to select not the guardian option.

After you have accepted the invitation, the person who invited you as well as the student is going to get an email alerting them that you have accept it and are now going to be getting email updates.

Whenever an email summary won't be sent

There are times that you are not going to get an email update and those times are going to be:

- When there is no activity to be reported for that period of time.
- Your student's teacher has notifications off for that class.
- You have chosen not to recieve summaries
- You are not connected to a student in that classroom.

Managing email summary settings

In order to manage email summaries you are going to need a Google account as we described earlier. Having a Google account is going to allow you to:

- View any student that is connected to your account
- Set up the frequency in which you get emails
- Update your location

Ito manage your email settings you will

1. Create a Google account if you have not already.
2. Sign into that account.
3. Move to your email and go to the bottom of your summary and click on settings.
4. Sign into the email settings page.
5. Enter your account email and select the next button.
6. Enter your password and sign into your account.
7. If you move to the frequency button you can change how frequently you recieve emails, if you do not want any emails, then select the no summaries option.
8. Under the time zone setting you can choose which time zone you reside in.
9. To look and see what email summaries you are going to recieve you will look under the Google classroom email summaries tab.

Unsubscribing from summaries

Email summaries can be unsubscribed from at any time. Keep your Google account so that you can reconnect with your student if you want to.

1. Once again, if you have not already created a Google account, you are going to want to.
2. Go to the bottom of your email and select unsubscribe.

Note: if you are a guardian, this is going to remove you from your students account as guardian if you are not using a free Google account.

Chapter thirteen: Extending Your Classroom

Getting the Classroom application

Whether you are a student or a teacher, you will have the option of installing the Classroom app on Android, Chrome, or App devices. This app is not currently available on Windows devices. If you are using a desktop, you will go to the Classroom website and log in.

After getting the app, you will sign in either as a teacher or as a student. As a teacher you are going to be able to manage your classroom from wherever you are.

Downloading the app

Android

1. Go to Google Play.
2. Locate the Google Classroom app and download.

iOS

The Google classroom app can be downloaded on an iPhone or iPad.

1. Go to your app store.
2. Install the Google Classroom app.

ChromeOS

The app is going to be like a bookmark on the internet. You can also go to the Chrome Web Store and download it from there.

Managed devices

In the event that your students school uses devices that are managed, the student may not have the option of installing the app themselves.

Should you be a teacher at a school that uses managed devices, you are going to have Google play for education access.

If you can get access from your admin console, you can then get the app sent out to your students so they can download it. You will also have the ability to send Google Drive and doc apps.

If you cannot get access, then you need to contact your school's administrator.

Chapter fourteen: Installing the Chrome Extension for Google Classroom

Both teachers and students that are using a chrome browser to access Google Classroom, you can share pages with the "share to classroom chrome extension". As a teacher, you can also use the extension to post announcements or assignments.

Who has the ability to install the extension

- Administrators: any administrator will be able to install the extension for any member that works for them.this is going to make it to where there is not as much time having to trouble shoot requests and makes sure that both teachers and students can instantly get started with the extension.
- Students: a teacher can post installation instructions in their class which enables the student to install the extension.
- Teachers: will get the ability to install the extension from their admin.

Admin install instructions

You will only be able to use G Suite for Education to preinstall the extension for those who fall under them.

1. Sign into your admin console.
2. Go to device management.
3. Move on to chrome management and then user settings.
4. Choose which unit you want to modify the settings for. Should you decide to change the settings for everyone, you need to select the top level unit or one of the child units.

5. Find the apps and extensions section which is going to be next to the force installed apps and extensions. You are going to need to choose the manage force installed apps.
6. Move on to the web store for chrome and search for share to classroom.
7. Now go to the extension and select add then save.

Teacher install instructions

1. First you are going to go to g.co/sharetoclassroom
2. Now you will select add to chrome.
3. Then click on add extension. You should see the share to classroom button at the top right of your address bar.
4. When you share to classroom an extension is going to be opened. Note: you are going to need to be signed into chrome in order to use the extension.

Posting installation instructions for your students

1. Select this link: https://classroom.Google.com/share?url=https%3A%2F%2Fg.co%2Fsharetoclassroom&body=Open%20the%20following%20link%20to%20install%20the%20Share%20to%20Classroom%20Chrome%20extension&title=Install%20the%20Share%20to%20Classroom%20Chrome%20extension
2. Pick which class you want to share the link to.
3. Select what type of post by clicking on choose action.
4. Select an option
   a. Make an announcement
   b. Create assignment
   c. Ask question
5. Pick the go button. A post is going to be opened with the instructions on how to add the attachment.

6. Select an option that will go with the instructions that you post.
    a. Select post if you are posting an announcement
    b. Click assign if you are posting an assignment
    c. And pick ask if you are asking a question
7. You can pick the view button in order to see what is being posted in the class stream.

Installation instructions for students

You are going to install the extension from the instructions that your teacher posted to your class stream.

1. Sign into your classroom with the Google account you created.
2. Go to your class.
3. Find the post that says share to classroom – chrome web store.
4. Add to chrome.
5. Add the extension. A share to classroom icon will appear at the top right of your screen next to your address bar.
6. Select this icon and you are going to open the extension. Make sure that you are signed into chrome before you do this.

Chapter fifteen: Using Screen Reader with Classroom

If a teacher or a student is blind or has low vision you are going to be able to use a screen reader on the computer or mobile device that is going to make it easier for them to see what is on the screen.

Web

Classroom can be accessed through the internet using a screen reader. You have the option of using any browser that you want and you are going to have to follow the instructions set forth by that browser on how to set up the screen reader. If you are using a Mac you can use voice over with your screen reader.

Mobile

Android

The Android Classroom app is going to work with the talkback application that is going to be preinstalled with the screen reader. Talkback uses spoken feedback for its interaction.

iOS

Just like Android uses talkback, iOS is going to use voiceover.

Chapter sixteen: Google Classroom API

Technology companies are working with schools to use Classroom API in order to build the tools needed to interact with the G suite and classroom so that they work better to meet the needs of the teacher and their students. API is a Google developer API which means that any non Google service is going to be able to benefit from the tools and infrastructure offered by Google.

In order to use the classroom API, the developer is going to need to agree to the API terms of service. Other applications are not going to be able to use data collected from Google Classroom for any advertising purposes.

Who can use classroom API

Any third party developer or administrator is going to be able to use Classroom API. Students and teachers are going to have the option to authorize third party applications so that they can use API as well.

What can you do with API

When using API you will have the ability to program things that typical students and teachers will use through the classroom UI. For example, you will have the option of synchronizing your student information so that you can see the classes that are being taught in that domain and then manage the classwork that is required for that particular class.

If a non Google service is using the API to integrate features that will be used with classroom, they may be able to do things such as allow the teacher to copy and reuse things that they used in their classroom so that they do not have to go back and recreate everything. Applications are also going to be able to modify the work in the classroom as well as add material, turn in work, and send back grades.

Applications and classroom data

Apps and services have access to the data that comes from a Google Classroom. However, apps are going to need to get authorization from the user before it uses data. App will typically ask for specific pieces of information to collect. As the user, you can agree to share the data or not. When authorizing the app to use data it is going to use Oauth which is a common standard to be used over the internet for authenitcating the approval to collect data.

G Suite for Education Admins

If you are an administrator in G Suite then you are going to be allowed to control just how much data you allow to be shared inside of your domain. From the admin console, you will specify who you want to authorize the services so that data can be accessed. You also have the ability to configure the access that is given by the organizational unit.

Also inside of the admin console you will have the option of looking at the services that are going to be granted access to an account in your domain so that you can remove privileges if needed.

Classroom API for users

There are particular tasks that can be done by Classroom API depending on what role the user occupies. Just like with the classroom UI, the user is going to be an administrator, teacher, or student. The teachers and students are going to be able to approve of any third party applications that need to be approved as well as report abuse inside of the classroom.

So, what can API do for you?

Student:

- Look at the details of the course and the teacher of that course.

Teacher:

- Create and modify classes.
- Set grades.
- Create assignments.
- Return work.
- View and modify class roster.

Administrator:

- Create and modify classes in G Suite.
- View work being done in classes.
- Add or remove students and staff from domain.

Chapter seventeen: Students and Their Google Classroom

You will sign into your classroom from your G Suite account or your personal Google account. Once you have signed in, you are going to be able to update the profile picture that is being used with your classroom profile or you can manage your password and settings for your Google account.

Signing into a Google classroom

You can use a G Suite for Education account or you can use a personal Google account.

Signing in

1. Go to classroom.Google.com and click on sign in
2. Enter your log in information before clicking on next.

Keep in mind that your Suite username is going to use a .edu email while your personal account will use a .com email.

3. Enter your password before signing in.
4. Should there be a welcome message, you are going to want to read it and then accept the terms and conditions.
5. If you are using a G Suite account, select that you are a student
6. Choose the get started button

Trouble signing in

If you are having this problem, there are several things that you may be able to do. Let's look at each situation and solution for that problem.

1. Your service is disabled by the admin.

This means that the classroom has not been activated for the account that you are using. What you need to do is contact your teacher or the school administrator to have them activate the classroom for you.

2. The classroom is only available for Education users only.

This means that you have tried to use a personal account instead of a school account. What you are going to have to do is go to your web browser and sign in with your education account. If you are using the mobile app you are going to need to use a different account to sing in with your education account.

Another issue could mean that your school is not using the G Suite for Education. If this happens, then your school needs to sign up for G Suite before Classrooms can be accessed.

3. Your administrator hasn't activated Classroom.

To use this classroom you need to contact your school's IT or G Suite Admin to activate the classroom. Your school is not using G Suite and to fix this issue you will need your school to sign up for G Suite.

Accessing classroom

By going to the menu, you can access other parts of Google Classrooms.

- Settings: you can change your passwords, notifications, and profile picture.
- Classes: you can look at all your classes that are using Google Classrooms.

- Work: see all of the assignments and posts associated with the assignment.
- Calendar: look at assignment due dates, test days, so on and so forth.

Managing classes

You are either going to get an email to join a class or get an access code from your teacher. Once you have joined you are going to see the class stream where you are going to be able to locate class resources.

Joining a class

In order to get into the Google Classroom that your teacher creates, you are going to need to sign into your classroom account and then join your teacher's class. There are two different ways to join a class as we have discussed throughout this book.

Your teacher can give you a code, you will use this code to add yourself to the class. Or, you are going to get an invitation in your email and you will need to select join that appears on the class card.

If you get deleted from the class or you lose or forget the class code, you can ask your teacher to give you a new code.

Note: you are only going to need to enroll once, once you have enrolled, there is not going to be any need for you to reuse the code.

Using a code to join the class

1. Go to Google Classrooms.

2. Go to the top and click the plus sign where it says join class.
3. In the box insert the class code that was given to you by the teacher before hitting join.

Accepting an invitation

1. Go to the Google Classroom website.
2. Go to the class stream and select join.

Note: the teacher is the only person who can change the image for the class, but you can change the profile picture for your classroom.

Withdrawing from a class

When you no longer need to be enrolled in a class, you can remove the class so your current classes remain organized. Teachers may archive their class but not all of them will do this. Therefore, you can withdraw from the class when you sign into Classrooms. But, you are still going to have access to your files from that class.

1. Go to Google classroom.
2. Move to the class card and select the more menu before clicking unenroll.
3. Confirm your unenrollment.

Viewing archived classes

When a teacher archives a class it is going to be moved to a new area in your classroom account. After the class is archived, you can still view the class and all of its material but you cannot submit or delete any of the material.

Once the class has been restored, you will be able to interact with it like you were able to before it was archived. However, if it gets deleted, your class is going to be permanently deleted.

Note: archived or deleted classes will still allow you to see the class files located on Google drive.

1. Go to Google Classrooms.
2. Go to the menu and choose archived classes.
3. Click on the class that you are wanting to look at.

Note: a teacher is the only person who can delete a class, if you want to leave the class you will need to unenroll from the class.

Viewing your classes resource page

Teachers can add resources for you to to use which are going to store information like the policies for the class, how they grade things, so on and so forth. There is also going to be a link to your teacher's email address and a link to the folder for that class on Google Drive.

1. Go to the about section.
2. Click on the item that you are wanting to view.

Viewing assignments on the calendar

You will be able to track the assignments and questions that have due dates on a class calendar. Therefore, your teacher is going to make an assignment in the class which will automatically be placed on the calendar for both the classroom calendar and the Google calendar. On your class calendar, you are going to see the due dates for assignments as well as any events that are coming up.

Viewing assignments due dates

1. Go to the menu at the top of the page.
2. Choose calendar.
3. Choose which assignment you want to open.
4. Click on next to look at past and future work.
5. Choose all classes to see work for all your Google classes.

Viewing class events

1. Go to your class.
2. Move to the about section.
3. On calender click on open in Google calendar.

Now you can see upcoming tests or field trips.

View work

You are going to be able to view your work on any class card that is located in your stream or you can go to the work tab in your Google classroom.

Upcoming work

Any unfinished or upcoming work that is due for that week will show up on your class card.

1. For every class you are going to see the upcoming work work and the due date that goes along with that assignment.
2. Click on the title to see all the instructions.

Work in the class stream

1. Go to your class.

2. Select the title for any instructions or feedback that may be attached to it.
3. In order to add a comment click on the add class comment or number class comment located at the top of the page.
4. Sending your teacher a private comment will be done by clicking on add private comment.

Viewing work on work page

1. Go to the menu and then go to work.
2. Select the title you want to look at.
3. Click add class comment to comment on something.
4. Click add private comment to send a private comment to your teacher.
5. Any work that you have already submitted can viewed by clicking on the done button at the top of the page. If the teacher has already graded the work, then there is going to be a grade with that assignment.

Answering questions

Teachers are going to be able post questions in their classes stream and the student is going to have the option of answering them. The questions are going to be able to contain attachments to files or videos.

Answering short answer questions

1. Pick the class you have a question to answer in. The question is going to appear in your stream.
2. If an attachment is there, then you will need to click on it and review it before submitting your answer.
3. Enter your answer and hit the submit button. You are going to need to hit confirm before your answer is sent.

The submit button is not going to be visible if you have not put an answer in.

4. You can send comments or private comments if you need to to get clarification on your question.

Note: your teacher may make it to where you can see how your classmates answered the question once you have submitted your answer.

Multiple choice questions

1. Go to the class.
2. Look at any attachments that may be there.
3. Pick which answer you think is suitable for the question and click submit.

Viewing and replying to answers by classmates

For the short answer questions, your teacher may make it to where you can see and even reply to the answers that your classmates submitted after you submit your answer. If your teacher does not turn this permission on, then you are not going to have this option. But, if you do, you can click on the see classmates answers on your question once you have submitted your answer.

1. Go to your class.
2. Go to the see classmate answers on the question.
3. Reply to any classmates answer by hitting reply and then posting that reply.

Editing your answer

For the short answer questions you may be able to edit your answer once you have submitted it. But, this is only going to work if your teacher allows for that permission to be turned on.

1. Go to your class.
2. Find the question and select the edit button.
3. Make your changes and hit submit once again.

Viewing returned work

A teacher can return any work that they want you to look at again and you are going to be able to view it on the work page or in your class stream. The work may not be graded when it is returned and this is going to be done so that you can edit the assignment and then turn it back in.

Viewing returned work on the work page

1. Go to the menu and select the work tab.
2. Select done to see what has already been submitted and graded. If there is any work that has been graded, then it is going to have a grade next to it.
3. You can sort your work out by class by going to the all classes filter and choosing a class to view.

View work in class stream

1. Go to the class that you want to view.
2. Select work and if you see a grade, then that assignment has been graded.

Writing notes on your work

There are tools in the Google classroom that make it to where you can add drawing and writing tools on your assignments. Words can be underlined, highlighted, shapes drawn, and notes left. You also have the option of drawing and writing on Adobe files, PDF files, Google Docs, and Microsoft Office documents.

Note: these tools are only going to be available when using the app on Android or Apple iOS.

1. Go to the classroom icon on your browser.
2. Go to your class and choose your assignment.
3. Look at the file if there is one attached.
4. If you need to create a new PDF you will open a blank file and write out anything that needs to be on that file.
5. Notes can be made with the drawing and writing tools.
6. Click the save icon to save your notes.

Note: you have to make sure that you are saving your work because the changes are not going to be saved automatically. If you leave the screen then you are going to lose your work.

7. You can open your work in Google drive by opening a new tab.

Saving notes

Should the original file be an image or a PDF file, the editing the file is going to overwrite the original file.

If the file is an office document or a Google docs file, the file you edit will be saved as a PDF.

Adding web pages to your assignments

Should you see the share to classroom button on a page, you will be able to use the button to post the web page on the assignment in your classroom. The share to classroom icon is going to usually placed next to social media icons.

Should a page not have this icon, then you can still submit the web page by using the URL.

1. Click the share to classroom icon.
2. Sign into your classroom.
3. Pick which class you want to share the URL on. You have to make sure that there is an upcoming assignment in that class.
4. Pick the assignment you want it attached to.
5. Hit the go button.
6. Attach the link.
7. View your assignment.

Connecting with your class

In order to connect with your classmates is to post on the class stream. You will also be able to see class announcments and take part in class discussions. If you need help from your teacher, you can email them directly.

Posting to the class stream

You can share things with your class or comment on things that they post in the class stream unless the teacher has removed this permission. All of the posts and comments made by any student is going to be visible to the entire class.

Ways to post

- Reply to a comment
- Create a new post
- Add a comment to someone else's post
- Add a comment to any post made by the teacher

Creating a post

1. Go to the class.
2. Move to the bottom and click the plus button then select create post.
3. In the box you will type in your message.
4. You can attach files if you need to.
5. If you are not wanting to post then hit the button that says cancel.
6. Post your comment.

Adding a comment to a post

1. Go to the class.
2. Find the post and click on the add class comment which is located on the post.
3. Enter your comment and post.
4. If you do not want to post your comment, then hit the cancel button.

Replying to a comment

1. Find your class in Google Classrooms.
2. Hover over any comment that you want to reply to and click on the reply button. The person that you are replying to is going to be mentioned automatically.
3. Put your comment in the box and post

Deleting posts and comments

When a post is deleted, all the comments will be deleted along with it. You are not going to be able to undo this action.

1. Go to your class
2. Find the post or comment and click on the more button.
3. Then go to delete and make sure you confirm it so that you can get rid of it.

Mentioning classmates in posts

Should you want to mention someone in a post in your classroom you can use the plus button or the at symbol along with that person's email. Both your classmates or teacher can be mentioned in a post or comment or even comment replies so that you can add them to the discussion or so that they can see what you wrote.

Whenever someone is mentioned they are going to get emails and you are going to receive emails too, but only if the notifications are on for their account settings.

The plus sign or the at symbol is only going to work when posting in the class stream.

+ mentions

1. Go to that class.
2. Insert your message in the comment box. Or your post in the new post box on the main screen.
3. Insert your mention before typing the person's name and choosing the name from the autocomplete list that appears.

4. If you want to pick a different name, go down the list until you find that person and then select enter.
5. Post your comment or post.

Note: if the name that you want is not appearing, then you are going to need to enter the entire email address for that person.

Viewing comments

Go to your gmail to see any notifications about comments that are posted in the class stream.

Replying to comments

You can reply to comments or posts in the class stream by going to that post or comment and entering in your own comment.

Sending emails

When using classroom from personal Google accounts your administrator may make it to where your contact sharing has been disabled which will make it to where you will not see the email button next to the names of your teacher or classmates.

Emailing a teacher

1. Go to the class of the teacher that you are wanting to email.
2. Move to the about section.
3. Under the teacher's name to the left is going to be an email button. Click on it and a new email box will appear on your screen.
4. Type in your email and hit send.

Emailing students

1. Go to the class that you share with that student.
2. Go to the classmates tab.
3. Find the name of the student and click on the three dot menu then choose email classmate. A message box is going to be opened.
4. Write out your message and send it.

Sharing a web page with a teacher

If you are using the chrome browser, then you will have the option of sharing a web page from the computer to the teacher's computer via the classroom chrome extension. This extension allows your teacher to send web pages back to you.

Sharing a web page with your teacher

The extension must be enabled on your computer as well as your teacher's computer so that you can share with each other. If you do not have the extension or are not sure if you do, then ask your teacher about it.

1. In the browser, go to the address bar and locate the share to classroom button.
2. Sign into your classroom account.
3. Find the name of your teacher's class and click on it.

Note: should you not have any classes joined, you will need to join an open class.

4. Select the push to teacher button, you are going to instantly be sending a message to your teacher with the web page you are wanting to share.

View recently shared pages

1. Go to the address back and click on the share to classroom icon.
2. Find the name of your teacher's class.
3. Go to the websites that you want to view.
   a. Received from teacher: these are web pages that your teacher sent you
   b. Pushed to teacher: these are the web pages that you sent your teacher

The web pages are going to automatically update whenever you send something to your teacher these pages are going to vanish after a certain period of time. You are not going to be able to remove these pages yourself.

Filtering your class stream

In the class stream you can see that the posts are going to be arranged by the time that they are posted. The most recent post is always going to appear at the top of the stream. If at any time your teacher creates topics, you are going to be able to filter your stream by these topics. If there are no topics created, then you will not be able to do this.

1. Select the class you want to enter.
2. Choose one of the options
   a. Go to a post and click on the topic to filter out for that specific topic.
   b. On the left there is a topics button that you can click and then select which topic you are wanting to view on your stream.

Chapter eighteen: The Drawing and Writing Tool

Choosing a tool

These tools can be located at the bottom of the app screen.

- Add text: add in a text note to your file.
- Write: draw or write lines with a writing device. The pressure is going to determine how wide the lines are.
- Erase: a note will be erased.
- Mark: a marker will be used to edit the file.
- Select: a note will be selected to move it or change its size.
- Highlight: images and text will be highlighted.

Changing the color or size

When writing, highlighting, or marking you can change the size ad color of the tool.

1. Pick a tool by tapping on it.
2. Change the color or size by using the up arrow.

Adding text notes

1. Click on the add text button.
2. Move your finger over the file so you create a new text field.
3. Insert your message.
   a. Tap a corner of the box to resize it.
   b. Use two fingers and pinch apart to make the text bigger.
   c. Use two fingers and pinch together to make smaller.

Erasing marks

1. Select the eraser.
2. Tap on a mark to erase it.
3. Double tap the eraser to remove all of the marks that are on the page.

Resizing or moving a note

1. Pick the select tool and tap on the note or image.
2. Use two fingers to pinch together or apart to resize.
3. Drag the note where you want it to be when moving it.

Zooming in and out

Use two fingers and pinch fingers apart to zoom out.

Use two fingers and pinch together to zoom in.

Drag your fingers over the screen to pan across the screen.

Undo or redo

Tap the undo button to cancel the action. Hit it multiple times to undo multiple actions at once.

To redo the action, hit the redo button. Hit it several times to redo the action.

Conclusion

Thank you for making it through to the end of *Google Classroom*, let's hope it was informative and able to provide you with all the tools you need to achieve your goals whatever it may be.

The next step is to decide if Google Classroom is right for your class. You are going to have the ability to keep everything organized and you are not going to be losing things like you might typically do.

As you saw demonstrated in this book, Google Classroom is going to be good for most classes because you are going to be able to communicate with the students and teachers even outside of school. On top of that it is going to be easily accessible and you are going to be saving time in using it.

In the end, as the world of technology and education evolves to meet the needs of those that are using it, you are going to see that Google Classroom is going to be used more and more so that classes are taught more effectively.

Finally, if you found this book useful in any way, a review on Amazon is always appreciated!

Thank you and good luck!

Google Classroom

Best Google Classroom Guide for the Student

Introduction

Congratulations on downloading your personal copy of *Google Classroom: Student Guide to Google Classroom.* Thank you for doing so.

The following chapters will discuss some of the many things that you are able to do with Google Classroom. This is a great feature that is available through Google, a software that a lot of people are familiar with using in their daily lives. While many people are able to use Google to help with their personal email, but there is so much more that can come with Google Classroom, which is why a lot of teachers are turning to this software to help to get more out of your courses.

There are a lot of different things that you will be able to do when you use Google Classroom and it is one of the best tools that students and teachers alike are able to utilize. Students will be able to ask questions in real life, set up their calendars, finish assignments and get instant feedback, and even work with some other people on a project all from any location that they would like. This guidebook is going to take some time to talk about all of the cool things that you are able to do when you are a student who uses Google Classroom for your courses!

When you are ready to learn more about Google Classrooms so that you can get the most out of all your hard work and you can keep all of your classes organized, make sure to read through this guidebook and get all of the information that you need to get started.

There are plenty of books on this subject on the market, thanks again for choosing this one! Every effort was made to ensure it is full of as much useful information as possible. Please enjoy!

Chapter 1: Google Classroom

When it comes to succeeding in the classroom, you want to make sure that you have some of the best tools around to get you ahead. And while there are many different programs and software that you can use and that promise to be the very best, Google Classroom is one of the best options for you to use. This guidebook is going to take the time to explain how Google Classroom works and why it is the best option for students!

Some of the things that we will discuss in this guidebook in regards to Google Classroom include:

- What is Google Classroom?
- How to manage your Google Classroom
- How to get the Google Classroom all set up as a student
- Things that students are able to use Google Classroom for.
- How to work with the Assignment Flow
- Other ways that students are able to use Google Classroom.

Google Classroom is one of the best products around to help students and teachers interact together to make the classroom something really unique. When you are ready to see how Google Classroom can help you as a student, make sure to read through this guidebook to get started!

There are a lot of great programs out there that you can use to help manage your courses and keep things on track. If you have attending school for any length of time, you are most likely familiar with at least a few of these classroom tools to get things done. Teacher's like to work with a wide variety of software to help share grades, do tests, and share other links that will help out in the classroom. In some cases, you will use the same program a few times, but often as you go through different years of school, you will find that the program is going to change all of the time.

But one option that you may notice as really popular in classroom management programs is Google Classroom. This one can be really beneficial because it is free to anyone who has a Google account (which can also be set up and maintained for free). Many people throughout the world already have a Google Account to send emails, to be on YouTube, or for a host of other reasons, so it makes it really easy for a teacher to invite their students to the Classroom without having to worry about other costs or issues that come up with some of the other classroom management systems.

Google is a name that most people are familiar with and many will already have a personal email account with them because it is free and doesn't require them to look at a lot of ads all of the time. You can get a lot of the same benefits that you know and trust from a regular Google account, but with more features and security when you use it as Google Classroom.

What does Google Classroom do?

With all of the other classroom management systems out there, you may be wondering why Google Classroom would be the choice that a lot of teachers will stick with. There are quite a few things that Google Classroom is able to do and it is one of the easiest systems to work with, which is one of the reasons that it is so popular. Some of the basic things that you will be able to do when you work with Google Classroom includes:

- You can use the email that is available through Google. You can use this to search for any of the important messages that are related to school, without having to worry about any delays or even ads that are found on some of the other popular email systems.

- Teachers are able to streamline what goes on in their classrooms by creating new assignments, sharing these assignments with the students in the class, and then grading these assignments without having a lot of things to worry about in between.

- Students will be able to collaborate with their teachers using Google Docs. You will also be able to create as well as edit docs and spreadsheets in this system and you can even create your own presentations in the browser with all of the changes being automatically saved. It is even possible to have several people work on the project all at the same time.

- The cloud storage that is available makes it easier to share and save your work and can make it easier for you to access these saved files no matter where you are. This can save you some hassle when it comes to sending attachments or worrying about merging the different versions if you work on them in different locations.

- You can also save your calendars on Google Classroom. This makes it easier to plan for the projects you need to work on and you can integrate your schedule on this calendar so that everyone can pick a time that works for them. You can also integrate these schedules with your hangouts, contacts, email accounts, and your Drive.

- You can even create a new website that you are able to use inside the class. This is something that can be useful based on the project or the event that you are working on inside of the Classroom.

- The Google Classroom even makes it easier for you to conduct some face to face meetings through video calls. This makes it much easier for you to get questions answered quickly rather than waiting around to hear back through email. It is also a great way for the teacher to create some virtual field trips if the location is too hard to get through.

- Archiving is another option that is popular with Google Classroom. You are able to archive the different emails and chats that happen in the Classroom, making them easier to go through later on.
- There are also a lot of add-on apps that you are able to use with Google Classroom. Some of the popular ones that are often used include Google+, Blogger, and Google Groups.

As you can see, there are quite a few things that you are able to do when it comes to using Google Classroom. Since there are many options to choose from, the program is free, and anyone is able to get on it, it is likely that in the present and in the future, many of the classrooms that you attend will use Google Classroom to share information and to get things done.

The difference between Google Classroom and your personal account

At this point, you may be curious to know what will make Google Classroom different from your own personal account. Mainly, Google Classroom was designed for educational purposes. It doesn't cost anything for either the teachers or the students to use, it can save a lot of time each week if you use the features properly, and you will have a lot of support to make sure that everything works well. There is also additional space and access to your Calendars, Google Docs, and Google Drive along with some great security features. One big reason that a lot of schools like to use Google Classroom is that in addition to all of the great features that come with it, they are also able to use the professional email domain name from their school.

In most cases, if you just want to send out emails with your Google Account, you will be just fine with using your own personal account. But if you are looking to join a classroom and want to be a part of all the extra apps and features that come with it, a Google Classroom account is much better. It can get hard to keep track of all your classes and the information that goes with them if you send this to your personal email, but with Google Classroom, it will all be in one place for you to find it pretty easily. Even if you have more than one teacher who is using Google Classroom, you will be able to find different sections for all of those classes and it won't be such a mess trying to search for the classroom and the right information all the time.

Both accounts will allow you to do a lot of cool things with Google and can help you to get access to some of the different features that come with Google, but Classroom is so much better for students and for teachers who want to work together and get thigs done for the class. Yes, you could use your Gmail account to help you to get started on this and to give you some of the same results, but if you have multiple classes that are doing this or you are trying to collaborate with other students to get the work done, you will find that it may not be the best option for you. Google Classroom is one of the best options to help you to get things done inside your classrooms.

Getting the Google Classroom App

Before you are able to go through and start using the Google Classroom, it is time to download the App that will make it all possible. Downloading the app can be pretty simple. You just need to go to either the App store or Google Play and then do a search for Google Classroom. Once you have this downloaded, you will want to choose whether you want to sign in as a student or a teacher. It is also possible for you to download an extension or an app that will work on the web, as long as you are using Google Chrome. You just need to go into the Chrome Store. If you would like to install this, you would need to use the following steps to make it happen:

1. Go to g.co/shared classroom.
2. Click Add to Chrome > Add
3. Click the icon that is right next to the extension. You will want to make sure that you are already signed in with Google before doing this step.

It is also possible to use the Google Classroom Screen Reader if you want a chance to keep things organized. In order to use this, use the following steps:

- Sign into your Classroom by going to classroom.google.com and then select that you are a student.
- You can then go to the Classroom Menu before pressing Enter.
- At this point, you are able to navigate to any of your classes (if you have more than the one you are working on at a time), manage your preferences, and also get a look at your assignments.

From here you should have the Google Classroom set up and you will be able to take a look at the classes that are on here. You are able to be signed up for more than one class at a time through the Google Classroom so you will need to make sure that you pay attention to which class you are in when reading messages and looking at the assignments that you are supposed to work on.

When you need to join a new classroom, your teacher will send out an invite to the one that they have created. At times you will notice that you are linked up with other classrooms too if the teacher has opened up these permissions so that everyone can work together. Once you provide your teacher with the right email address and you are invited to join in on the classroom, you will be able to use all of the features that are available through that particular classroom, such as interacting with the other students, sending emails, seeing the calendar and the assignments, and so much more. This is a great way to keep all of your classes together and organized and it doesn't take too much effort to get everything all set up.

Chapter 2: Managing Google Classroom

Before we go much further, it is important to realize that the Google Classroom API is the thing that is going to make this feature work the way that you would like. This part is going to let technological companies and schools work in order to create the best apps that students and teachers will be able to use in order to properly communicate with each other concerning different topics, assignments, and other issues with the class. It can even make the process of studying a little bit easier. Some of the topics that the Google Classroom API is going to cover include:

Managing Courses

When you are inside of your Google Classroom, a course is going to represent one "class". It can have any name that the teacher wants, but they will most likely give it a name that will help to distinguish it from the other classes that they are teaching. For example, you may see a class that is called Mrs. Johnson's 4th Period Science. This can make it easier for the student to go through and figure out which class they need when they are online.

The API for Google Classroom will be able to support the class and will include all of the assigned teachers, students, and even the metadata that goes with it. It is also going to be able to support:

- Developer project: this part is all about being able to manage some of the aliases that are given to the different applications. These aliases are then going to be tied over to the Google's Console Developer's Project.
- Domain: domains are important inside of this system because without having them there, it is hard to create

the specific addresses and aliases and without these, it would be difficult for both the students and the teachers to know what they should use or where they should go.

Managing the teachers and the students

With the help of the Google Classroom API, it becomes much easier for an administrator to differentiate between the students and the teachers. There may be some times when this differentiation can change. For example, there may be one course where a person is considered a student and another one is a teacher and then these roles can switch later on.

In the Google Classroom, the teachers are going to be the people who will be in charge of instructing in the course. They are able to view as well as change the course details. They will also be responsible for managing the flow of their course as well as for managing their students. On the other hand, the students will be the other people who are enrolled in this class. These students will be able to view the details of the course as well as have an idea of who the teachers are of the course.

The Google Classroom API makes it so much easier for you to manage the classroom that is needed to get things done. There are a lot of different options that you can work with inside of the Google Classroom and the teacher can personalize it to make sure that the student is able to get the most out of the experience and out of their learning. When all of the parts are able to come together, it is easier than ever to take care of what goes on in the classroom without wasting a lot of time.

In some cases, the administrator is going to be the school that holds onto the Google Classroom Account. They will be able to pick which teachers are able to be on the system and then they will assign the emails that are needed for each student. The students will be given their new emails when they start at the institution and then the teacher can get the list that goes with each class they set up. This can save some time and confusion and will make it easier for everyone to work together on the class.

Once the teacher has the access that is needed, they are able to create a different class for each of the courses that they run. They should make sure that they give them names that help keep things separate if they have several courses that are the same. For example, if they teach three courses of Algebra 1, they may want to name it with the time period that they teach each one, like Algebra 1 Period 3 and so on to keep things in order. The classes may receive the same information in many cases, but it will help the teacher to figure out who is in each class and to share the information properly.

After the teacher has had some time to set up the classes that they want to use, they can then use their link to send out invitations to the different students who should be in each class. If the educational institution provided emails to the students, the teacher can just go through and use these emails to find the students who belong to each of the classes. They can send out the invites to these emails and get all of the students to the right courses in no time.

In some cases, the educational institution will not go through and require a Google Classroom Account so the teacher will be able to set it all up on their own. They can set up the classes that they would like to use for this and then during class they can ask their students for the emails that should be used. As the teacher collects the emails, they will be able to send out these links to get the student to join. Or the teacher can get a code to the class and hand that out to the students, who can then go through and get into the class.

Once all of the students are in the class, it is so much easier to share information, work on projects together, and so much more. There are so many things that the teacher and the students will be able to work with together inside of Google Classroom and this area can be perfect whether you are just using this on the side with your regular classroom or if this is going to replace the regular classroom and you are taking everything online. It is so much easier for teachers to provide personalized learning to their students in ways that were just not possible before. With the help of discussions, assignments, and so much more, the student will be able to learn on the Google Classroom and get what they need out of every classroom.

Chapter 3: Getting Google Classroom Setup for Students

As a student, you are going to be impressed by all of the things that you are able to do with the help of Google Classroom. While teachers are going to be able to assign homework and invite you to the classroom, there are a lot of benefits that you will be able to get when you decide to use Google Classroom as well. The benefits are not just there for the teachers as students will like all of the options that are there for them to learn as well. This chapter is going to go over some of the things that students should know about using Google Classroom and getting it to work for them.

In this chapter, you will be able to take a look at how to get onto your own personal Google Classroom Account and how to set it up so that you are able to get into the classes that you will like. You are going to have just one Google Classroom Account to get on to all of your classes in one place. You can even see that your assignments are all going to be collected in one place because they will all connect to the same Calendar. When you are done with this chapter, you will be able to get into your account, sign up for your classes, and so much more with the help of Google Classroom.

Signing In

The first thing that you need to know how to do is how to sign in. If you aren't able to get onto the Google Classroom, it is going to be really hard to see which classes are available for you to do, submit assignments, work with some of the other students on some of your projects, or use the other neat features that are available with Google Classroom. Some of the steps that you need in order to sign into Google Classroom includes:

With a web browser

- To log in with a web browser, you would first need to visit classroom.google.com and then click on the student tab.
- Type in the credentials that your teacher has set up for you or the ones that you have from your own accounts.
- From here you will be able to go on a guided tour of the virtual classroom and learn how to use all of the neat tools that are there.

With an Android or iOS App

If you want to sign into Google Classroom with the help of a mobile app, this is possible, you would just need to go through and use the following steps to make it happen:

- Touch the icon that looks like a person.
- Now enter in all of the details that you have for your Google Apps for Education and then continue with signing in.
- Select Student before touching on submit.
- At this point, you will have a choice to either take a guided tour of the classroom or not. If you decide not to take this tour, you can click on Skip to miss out on it.

As you can see, you will find that it is pretty easy to join a class inside of Google Classroom. In most cases, you will just need to wait to get an invitation from your teacher for the class, which your teacher will be able to send out simply by having your email address. In some cases, the teacher will give you a code and you will be able to place that into the code box once you are signed into classroom.google.com. Both methods are easy to use and will ensure that you are getting into the right classes that you need in order to get all of your work done and to use all of the cool resources that your teacher has set up.

Viewing the Class Resource Page

Once you are added to a classroom, it is time to know what is going on in your particular class. You will want to have a good idea what this particular class is about and some of the resources that the teacher has made available for you to use. In order to view the resource page for your class, you would go through the following steps:

- Click on the class that you have joined If you are in more than one class, make sure that you are in the right one.
- From here, you will click on About and then choose the item that you would like to take a look at.

Depending on the class that you are working with, there may be a few different things that will show up inside of this part so look around and see what is available. This is a great way to become familiar with the class that you are working in and to make sure that you are able to find what you need later on.

Viewing an archived class

After you have finished with a class, such as when a class is over at the end of a semester or the school year, you are able to archive that class. This moves it out of the way but still has it around so you can see things that are in it for later on. If you find out later on that you need some of the information from a class or you would like to review some of the resources that were in that class after it has ended, you are able to check out your archived classes if you would like. In order to view these Archived Classes, you can do the following steps:

1. Click on your Menu and then select the button that says All Archived Classes.
2. Select the class that you would like to look at.

From here, you will be able to go through this class and get whatever information that you would like. You can look at some of the resources, the various projects you worked on and more. You will need to make sure that you archive all of your classes when they end so that you can get this information later on. You never know when you will need to get this information again so always be careful before deleting or doing other things to some of your old classes when you get done with them.

Any time that you would like to go through and see some of your own projects or some of the information that is in your other classes, such as when you would like to review an easier class before going into a more advanced class, you can use the steps above. The archived classes will stick around so that you are able to watch what is going on and get the information that you would like from each one whenever you need.

Viewing the class calendar

There are many times when you may need to take a look at the class calendar. This will let you know what assignments are coming up in the class when big tests will happen, and the other big events that the teacher adds into it. This can really be helpful for you to keep everything in one place and you won't have to always remember the dates all of the time. It is a great way to help you have an idea of what you should expect in class and what you are expected to do. In order to view your class calendar, you will need to use the following steps:

- Click on the Calendar button when you are in your Classroom Page.
- From here you can click on an assignment inside of the Calendar if you would like to know about a specific assignment, or you can click on Quick Question to have access to this information from your Student page.

- Then you can click on the arrow to have an idea of what is going on over the next week or more based on what information you need.
- If you would like to filter the events so that you can see something in particular. Lick on All Classes and then choose the class that you feel like filtering events for.
- This will then show you the information that you want to take a look at.

And that is all that you will need to do in order to look at some of the assignments that are coming due for your class. You can switch around between classes and look at the due dates for the various assignments that you need to get done with. This is a good way to take a look at due dates, tests, and other important dates that your teacher posts all in one location.

Setting up your mobile notifications

One of the options that you are able to work with is to set up some mobile notifications about your classes. This can be really helpful because it allows you to know right away when a new assignment or a new announcement is posted by your teacher. It can also show you when someone mentions you in a post or a discussion so that you can give an answer back. In some cases, it is going to help you to send and receive some private notes, correspond with others in your classroom, and will even provide you with a way to get your ratings and grades for assignments right away.

There are several different methods that you can use in order to set up these mobile notifications. To set these up for your iOS, you would need to use the following steps:

1. Touch the icon that looks like a person before touching on Settings, Notifications, and then Notifications again.

2. Choose to Allow Notifications at this point and then you can choose whether you want those notifications to be turned off or if you would like to turn them on.
3. If you want to see how many notifications you have, you can then go in and choose Show inside the Notification Center.
4. If you would like to have a certain sound come up when you receive a notification on your iOS device, you can turn on sounds at this time.
5. You can even go through and make it so that the notifications will show up even if you happen to have your screen locked. You just need to click on Show Notifications on Lockscreen to make this happen.

There are a few other alert types that you are able to choose from when working with this step on your iOS. You can choose to work with alerts, which will show your notifications right in the center of the screen. If you click on banners here you will see your notifications show up right on the top of the screen. If you click on none, you will need to swipe down so that you can see what notifications are there for you.

If you would like to be able to set up your notifications on your Android device, you would need to use the following steps to make it happen:

1. Here you will want to touch on the icon that looks like a person.
2. From here you can scroll down until you reach your settings, and make sure that you check on the vibration and the sounds if you would like to have these while you get your notifications.
3. Any time that you would like to turn off these notifications with your Android device, you just need to go back in and click the right buttons to make this

happen.

Getting notifications sent to your phone is pretty simple and can help you to have a good idea of what is going on in each of your classes. If you like to stay on top of your classes and you like to know ahead of time when a new test or project is due even if you are out and doing other things, setting up the notifications on your iOS or Android device can be pretty easy to accomplish. You are able to see these notifications when you log in to your student account, but in some cases, it is easier to have all of these notifications sent directly to your phone.

How to change your account settings

If you have a Google Classroom Account, it is possible to go through and change the settings so that it works the way that you would like. Sometimes you may only want to change one or two things about your account, and other times you will want to change quite a bit so that the account works the way that you would like. If you want to change the settings on your Google Classroom Account, this can be pretty simple to work on. You just need to go to the Classroom Page before selecting Settings. From here you are able to change any of the settings that you would like for that classroom. Some of the things that you are able to change in here include:

- See when someone tags you in a post or if they send you a comment.
- When there are some new assignments, or if the teacher has sent an assignment back to you.
- Whenever a teacher gives you a new grade for that classroom.
- Whenever someone sends you a private comment or message so that you are able to respond.
- Whenever a teacher posts out a new announcement or

assignment for the classroom.

As you can see, there are many different things that you are able to do when you work with your own Google Classroom. This chapter spent some time helping you to get started with setting up your account and getting organized so that you can start to get the most out of your classes. After you are done with this chapter, you are all set to start getting the most out of all the great features that are available with your Google Classroom.

Chapter 4: Things That Students Can Use Google Classroom For

Once you have had time to get into your Google Classroom and look at some of the different classes that you have available there, it is time to learn all of the things that you are able to do with the help of Google Classroom. While this may seem like a really simple tool for you to use, Google Classroom is really great at helping you to work on many projects and different assignments inside of the Google Classroom. It is the perfect companion to all of the different classes that you will want to use to make the most out of your learning experience. Some of the different things that you are able to do with the help of Google Classroom includes:

Sharing

While you are in your Classroom, you will be able to share with some of the other people who are in that class. You can go to the Stream tab in order to share your thoughts or even provide an answer so that the whole class will be able to see. Students are able to go through and share some other options with their messages as well including videos, web links, various files, and documents if they would like. This makes it really great for sharing information and sources to support the comments that you are making, such as in a discussion for the class, and others will be able to access the information to help them out as well.

In addition, the teacher will be able to add in some other links and documents to the classroom to help you to have the right materials and resources that are needed. The teacher will be able to share as much information that they need in order to help you complete your assignments, work on your tests, and so much more. This is a great way to share anything that you need throughout the classroom.

Assignments

It is easier than ever to work on the assignment when you use the Google Classroom. Students will not have any excuse for forgetting about their assignments or leaving them at home. They are able to access all of their assignments through the Classroom and they can easily look at the Calendar to see when the due dates are coming up. If the student would like to look at all of the assignments at the same time, they can just click on the View All button to help you out. The student will also notice that there are done and To-Do tabs and they can click on to help them mark the status of each of their assignments.

In addition, the student is able to add a new link, file, or document to their assignment box so that they upload papers or even videos if this is part of the assignment. If they want to make a comment on the assignment, such as to say it is done or something else, they can just press the button that says Add Comment near the bottom of their assignment. If you do post a comment in this area, remember that the comment is going to be public so anyone who is in the class will be able to see your comments.

Keep Track

One of the cool features that you are able to see with the assignments is that when the teacher assigns it and gives you a due date, you will see that it shows up automatically on the Google Calendar. If you see a new assignment and you are uncertain about the due date, you can just go onto the calendar and take a look. This is a good way for all students to be able to keep track and monitor the assignments that they have for each class. You can even color code your classes so that it is easier to see which assignments go with which class, all in one spot.

It is also possible for students to be able to see how their progress is going on each assignment. The Google Classroom is able to support what is known as the BYOD method, which makes it easier for the whole learning process and makes things easier for both students and teachers.

In some cases, you may want to work back and forth with the teacher to finish the assignment. You may have an essay that will need to be submitted in various steps to the teacher, such as the introduction an outline, and a few drafts. You will be able to use the tools with Google Classroom to go through and see where you are on the assignment and how far you still have to go based on the notes from the teacher and how many steps you have completed for that particular assignment.

Work on projects

Google Classroom makes it easier to work on projects as you would need to. The teacher can leave a little comment or the instructions that are needed for the project, and the student can go from there. There are many different types of projects that are doable with the help of Google Classroom including writing reports, working on videos, voice clips, presentations, and so much more. If you are able to send it over an email, you will be able to use it on your Google Classroom to share with the teacher.

There are a variety of project types that the teacher is able to set up for students to work on. Some of these projects are going to be all about doing an individual project to demonstrate what the student has learned. These can be like reports on a subject, discussion questions, or something else. The teacher can even watch the progress of the student and leave them some feedback as they go, helping them to learn as they are going and the student can fix some of the mistakes before they get too confused.

In other cases, the teacher may want to have a few students work together on a project to make things happen. This is also possible and Google Classroom makes it easy for students to work together, to see who has finished their particular part, and so much more. Students won't have to worry so much about getting the project done in class or about finding a time when it works for everyone to get together. You can each work on your part when there is some time and the whole project will get done without all of the hassle or the wasted time. This makes it so much easier for everyone to work together and to get things done.

One of the projects that the teacher will be able to use is to have students work in discussion groups. The teacher can put up a few questions that they want the students to read through and answer, and then the students can go on when they have some time to leave a response to the questions there, respond to other comments, and more. This is a great way to make sure that even the shy students, the ones who don't do well with speaking up in class, are able to leave some of their comments and it gives the teacher a good idea of where everyone stands in the class and whether they need to go over the material some more.

Feedback

Another thing that you will notice when working with the Google Classroom is that you will be able to comment back on a note that comes in on your assignment. If you don't understand one of the notes that your teacher left on your assignment or you want to ask a question, you will be able to respond back right there. You can ask questions or for clarification and the teacher will be able to get right back to you as well.

This makes it a much better learning environment compared to the traditional classroom since this is not something that can usually happen in the regular classroom. In a traditional classroom, the teacher will just check and return an assignment and often there isn't a chance to discuss some of the important parts that come with it. This means that the student is often left without a full understanding of where they went wrong or how they are able to improve. The teacher will be able to use the feedback section of Google Classroom to discuss the feedback and this will help the student to actually learn from their mistakes.

Other functions of Google Classroom for students

We have spent a lot of time talking about the various things that you are able to do with the help of Google Classroom. Not only does this make things so much easier for the teacher, but the students will be able to enhance their learning experience, interact with the other students inside of the classroom, ask questions without having to wait, and work on projects with others as well. This is a much better place to learn compared to the regular classroom, whether the teacher decides to use this to enhance the learning or to be the entire classroom.

But there are still some other functions that you are able to do with Google Classroom and the benefits to students just keep growing. Some of the other benefits that you will be able to use as a student who is on Google Classroom includes:

- Add some feedback to a lesson that is not really clear to you. This will help you to keep notes for asking questions later on or the teacher can look through them later and answer your questions to clear up the lesson. You can also save some of this feedback into a new folder so that you are able to revise it later on if needed.

- Send private messages to the teacher. This is a great tool to use if you have some questions to ask your teacher and you don't want to leave it in a comment that others are able to see.

- Create your own digital portfolio. If you create this, you should consider putting some of your projects and some of your best work into this portfolio so that you are able to find it later if you need to use this information or you would like to reference it later on.

- You can use Google Sheets in order to create as well as monitor your own growth in each class.

- Email some of the other students, either as a group if you are working on a project together or you can even message an individual student if you need to ask a question or you want to start a conversation for some other reason.

- Submit assignments that have attachments. There are many options that are available for you to use as attachments that go along with your assignments such as web links, videos, drive files, documents, and voice clips.

- You will be amazed at how much paper will be saved when you are using Google Classroom. You will even be able to eliminate the use of paper and you can copy your work or distribute it without having to worry about using real paper.

- Students are able to be held accountable for their homework and the due dates that are selected with it. The due dates are automatically going to be placed on Google Calendar so if you are confused about a specific assignment, you just need to go onto the Calendar and take a look at it.

- Students are even able to participate in something that is known as a read aloud. They can do this by replying to some of the questions that are posted in the Classroom. Students are also able to engage in accountable talk with the help of discussion groups, which helps to get more students involved, especially those who are not so good at speaking up in a large group n the traditional classroom.

- The Google Classroom app is pretty flexible and can be easy to access and manage for the teacher and the students. The student is going to be able to use this app to explore the different instructional materials that are placed in the classroom, which makes it much easier to learn from.

- While the Google Classroom is only going to be accessible for students who belong to the specific educational institution that is using it, anyone will be able to access some of the other apps through Google such as the spreadsheets, presentations, docs, and slides.

- Many people enjoy that Google Classroom is really mobile friendly. This means that you shouldn't have much problem with using this on a mobile device. You can use this to either get onto your Google Classroom to look at assignments, to work on projects, and to participate in discussions, or you can even set it up so that you receive notifications when things change inside the classroom.

- The classroom makes it much easier to promote some collaborative work amount teachers and the students who are in the classroom, much more than you would be able to find inside of a regular classroom. With the help of discussions, the ability to work on projects together, the comment features, and through feedback, the teachers, and the students are going to be able to work together to get things done and to enhance the whole learning experience.

While most people hear about Google Classroom and assume that this is just a tool that benefits teachers and doesn't provide much for the student, that is just not true. It is really helpful to many students in terms of keeping things organized and helping them to ask the questions and get the responses that they need to really enhance their learning. The powerful features that are found in Google Classroom make this a really efficient tool that aids students in the different aspects of learning whether you are looking to help with productivity, multitasking, and communication.

Moreover, most people know that assignments often take up the majority of the time that students spend in school, but when using the Google Classroom option, the assignment process is going to become much easier than before. The student is able to click on a button and then they will be able to access their assignments and then work on it, whether they are sitting at home getting the work done or have to do it while they are on the go. There is no need for heavy books, pens, and notebooks to finish the homework because all of this material is going to located inside the Classroom.

Another thing that you will love about Google Classroom is that it is going to automatically title the documents and the assignments from the student so that things don't get messed up and they don't have to search around to hopefully find the name that works for them. Anything that the teacher of this classroom ends up creating for the students will be shared automatically inside of the classroom. This makes it easier for the teacher to monitor all of the progress of the students while also leaving comments, which will make each student more accountable. This can help to make a more personalized plan for the students compared to what can be done in a regular classroom.

The Google App for education

In addition to using the Google Classroom, students are going to love that they are able to use some of the additional educational tools that are available from Google. These are known as Google Apps for Education. Basically, this is a free service that is available to those who are using Google Classroom and makes it much easier for the student to have all of the tools that they need in order to get the most out of their classroom. Some of the apps that are available through this service include Spreadsheets, Google Docs, Presentation, Gmail, and Google Calendar. All of there are necessary to enhance the learning process and these apps, as well as the storage, will be free if you are already using Google Classroom for your needs.

In addition, both the teacher and the students will be secure with their privacy and their account cannot be used without permission. Google Ads are not allowed when they do a Google Search through this to help make it a little safer for everyone to use. There are even some schools that have switched over to Chromebooks to make the experience a little bit better.

How do students like Google Classroom?

According to some of the online polls and surveys that have been done about Google Classroom, most students agree that this is a great tool to use. Everything for the classroom can be done in one place with ease and it is easy to do everything from joining the class, talking to others inside the class, and even submitting the assignment. Because of the benefit of unlimited storage, the materials and files that the student uses or uploads are going to be online and safe, and they are able to add in as much of their own material as they would like.

One of the biggest issues that a lot of students have with Google Classroom is that they feel they don't fully understand how to use the system or all of the things that they are able to do with the system. This is why Google has implemented a walk through when you first sign up to help you use that, and teachers should consider making this a part of their introduction to ensure that students are fully prepared to use the software and get the most out of their learning with this system.

There is just so much that students are able to do with Google Classroom and it is not just a tool that helps out the teacher. Both teachers and students are able to benefit from the help of the Google Classroom and learning how to effectively use it and to utilize all of the features that come with it will make it easier than ever to get the results that you are looking for in your learning experience. When you try out a few of the options and tools that are in this chapter, you are sure to learn some really cool things that will get you ahead with the help of your Google Classroom.

Chapter 5: The Assignment Flow

The next thing that we need to focus on here is how you will be able to work with the assignment flow inside of the Google Classroom. This is something that will help both the teacher and the student to understand so you will need to go through this section and make it work for you. There are likely to be a lot of different assignments that you will need to work on when you are in Google Classroom because this is a good way for the teacher to have a good idea of where you are in your coursework and whether you are grasping the material that they are giving you. If you are uncertain about how the assignments work, when they are due or even where to find them, you are not going to have much luck in the class

Remember that when a teacher first assigns a project, the due date is going to be placed on your Google Calendar. Google Classroom is able to sync together all of the classrooms that you have together so when you look at the Calendar, you will be able to see the assignments for all of the classes that you are in at that time. This is going to make things so much easier for you to work with because you won't have to scramble around or look at the different classes in order to get your due dates. You are even able to go through and change the colors that you want to use in each class so that it is easier to see where all of the assignments go on the calendar.

Now back to the assignment flow. The first step that is going to happen with the assignment flow is that the teacher will go into the classroom and then create an assignment. When that assignment is created, they will go through and attach it to a Google Doc file. This makes it easier for the student to go through and edit the copy of this assignment before they turn it in. If the assignment is an answer sheet or something like this, this is all the teacher will need to do. The teacher can even assign an essay and place a prompt at the top of the Google Doc file and then send it over. Or they can keep it simple and just attach the instructions for the assignment, such as the questions to answer or to go to a discussion and work, or even a certain amount of pages that they want you to read.

When an assignment is posted, it is going to be located inside of the classroom that you are in. You can go to the assignment tab to see what it is all about or you can look on the Calendar to get a good idea of when it is due and so on. Depending on the notifications that you set up for yourself, you may also receive a text message that a new assignment has been posted and an email sent to your Gmail account to make it easier.

After the student has been able to go through the assignment, fill in the document, and then turn it in, the teacher will receive the assignment. The teacher will be able to grade it right away if they are able to, or when they have some free time. When the teacher is done with grading the assignment or leaving some of the comments that they want for the assignment, they will be able to give it right back to the student.

This is something that is really nice with Google Classroom. The student will not have to wait weeks to hear back about how they did on a particular assignment. If they finish it early, the teacher is able to go through and grade it as soon as they can and submit the results back, helping the student to get almost instant feedback and to have a good idea on how they did with that assignment. The student will be able to see how they did and what they could do better in the future.

Remember that the teacher is able to leave comments on the assignment, but if the student is not able to understand why they got something wrong or they need a bit more clarification, they are able to ask right there on the assignment. This makes it easier for some instant feedback and learning with the teacher without having to waste valuable class time.

This system can even be used for tests and quizzes as well. The teacher can add these to the assignments and give the students a certain amount of time to finish it. If the test is given during class time, they can all sit and get the work done right then and there, but if it is a test that is given for at home, the teacher could set it to get done in a certain amount of days. The student will be able to get the test done and submit it right away. The teacher can grade it right away or they can use a Google Classroom add-on that can instantly grade the test for them. This makes it easy for the student to see their results and get instant feedback that is not always available when they are in the regular classroom.

There is a lot that you are able to expect when you use Google Classroom to help you get things done. Some of the things that both students and teachers are going to be able to expect from this system include:

- The set up is easy: setting up all of the assignments is an easy process. It is basically about signing in, creating the class if you are a teacher or finding the right class if you are a student and then getting into it. This system is set up to help you have more choices in the stuff that you are studying and the streamlined process is going to make it all easy as well.
- More organization: another thing that you are going to enjoy about working in Google Classroom is that it helps the student to keep really organized. You will be able to find all of the materials for that class filed in the Google Drive folders, and you can even seem them in the class stream. You won't have to spend a lot of time searching around for what you want to use in one place.

- Saves time and paper: with a workflow that is paperless, students will be able to better manage their work, without having to worry about making a mess.
- Secure and very affordable: Google has great security so you know that your information and assignments are going to stay safe and secure. And considering that Google Classroom, along with all of the apps and tools that you are able to use with it, is free, you won't have to worry about spending a lot of money to make it work.
- Better communication: you can expect that with using Google Classroom, you will have an easier time communicating with your teachers as well as with your peers in a way that you have never been able to do before.

While Google Classroom may seem like a simple tool that you will be able to use on occasion, it is actually something that is extremely effective at helping you to manage your workflow and learn as much as possible in a short amount of time. When you are ready to get started with your Google Classroom, just find the class that you belong to and dive right in!

Chapter 6: Other Ways Google Classroom Can Help You Succeed

This guidebook has spent a lot of time talking about the various ways that you can use Google Classroom to enhance all of your learning experience. There may be other programs that are similar and offer some of the same services, but none of them offer these services for free and none of them have the security and great products that you are able to experience when you are working with Google Classroom. This is really one of the best platforms for teachers and students alike to use for all of their needs.

In the previous chapters, you learned how to get into a class and how to get things all setup, and even about how you are able to share with others in the classroom to get your work done. You learned how to finish your assignments and to get almost instant feedback from the teacher about what went right and what you need to work with to improve your score. This helps you to learn more than you can in a traditional classroom. In addition to some of the things that have discussed so far in this guidebook, there are also a lot of other great ways that you can use Google Classroom to make your life a little bit easier. Some of the other things that you can consider doing with your Google Classroom Account includes:

Google Forms

One of the features that you can do with Google Classroom is to use the Google Forms. These make it really easy for the teacher to obtain information from their students and for the students to leave some feedback about assignments, the class and more. To keep this simple, the teacher would be able to set up a Google Form in order to open up responses from people in the class. They can ask some open-ended questions, send out a survey, or something else. When the student is done with the survey, it will be marked as complete so the teacher knows when the information is all complete.

Many times the teacher will use this as a way to provide their students with a survey at the end of the year. They can ask how the class worked, what things, if any, they would change, and so on. This is a great way for teachers to keep up with what is going on in their classrooms and to see if the work is really being that effective.

Google Calendar

The Google Calendar is all automated on the system so this makes it easier for students and teachers to keep track of the things that they need to work on when they are in a particular class. Whenever a teacher puts up a new assignment, project, test or another thing for the students to work on, the due date is automatically going to be placed and synced up with the Google Calendar. Students can easily go through and see when their assignments are due for all of their classes without having to search through all of the classes or spend a lot of time wondering when it is all due. The student also has the option to choose to sync together the dates that are on their Calendar with their email accounts or even with their mobile phones so they can get notifications when they are approaching a due date.

Use the About Page

One thing that a lot of students will forget to use is the About Page because they don't think that it is all that important for them. But filling out this About Page can be really good for everyone involved. For the teacher, it is a good idea to fill in the About Page with accurate information to help the student understand what class they are taking and who the teacher is. For example, the teacher may want to consider writing a good description of the particular class as well as links to your website, a little bit about you, and some of your contact information in case a student needs to get ahold of you.

In addition, your students can also go through and fill out an About Page as well. They can tell a little bit about themselves to introduce themselves to the other people in the class, share their interests, and so on. Teachers could choose to make this one of the assignments for the students to be a kind of ice breaker and to help them to learn a bit more about the students.

Reuse the posts

One of the nice things that a teacher will be able to do with Google Classroom is that they can take some of the posts that they used before, in another class or in a previous class, and then reuse them a bit. This can be announcements, assignments, and even questions from their previous classes to help them keep up with the work, especially if the information still works with this current class.

For the students, it is possible to go through and see some of the old classes that they were in. This can be helpful if you need to review something that is inside of the older class or you want to get ahold of some papers or discussions that you want to use from a past semester. You just need to go through some of your past archived classes to find what you would like.

Setting the theme

Some students go into their Google Classroom and leave everything the way that it is. They are happy with the theme and how everything is set up so they won't want to switch anything around. But if you would like to take your Google Classroom and set it up in order to have some personalization to it, you will be able to do that by changing some of the settings inside of Google Classroom. There are many different color palettes that you are able to choose from as well as different themes so you can mess around with this a little bit to find what works the best for your account. In order to set up a new theme that you want to use in the classroom, you can use the following steps:

- Open up Class
- From here, you can select the Theme button that is at the bottom of the image in your image settings.
- Now you can either select an image from the gallery or you can click on the Patterns button in order to pick out the theme that you would like.
- Once you have picked out what you would like to have there, you can click on Apply and the new theme is going to be all set up.

It is also possible to upload some of your own pictures to the gallery in order to use that when picking out the new theme that you are using.

Find conversation starters

This is one that the teacher is most likely going to work with, but as a student, you will be able to go through and see what conversation starters the teacher has posted for you. You should be on the lookout for these to see what the teacher is asking for, such as feedback on the recent announcements or even information about the discussion groups that you need to respond to for a grade. This is a fantastic way for you to keep everyone in the class united, even if they are all in different locations.

Send out emails

Since this is a Google program, you will be able to use the Gmail account to send out emails to other people in the class. The teacher will be able to choose whether to send out an email to individual students if they need to, or they can pick out groups of students that they need to share information with, such as new announcements for the whole class.

In addition, the students would be able to use the email system to talk to others inside of their Google Classroom. For example, if they need to ask the teacher a question and they don't want to post it on the open forum or discussion, they are able to send out an email to do this. They can also use their email to talk to individual students or to groups of students who are in the same classroom as well.

Check progress

While the student is working on the project the teacher will be able to check how well the student is doing simply by clicking on the Submission History. They can then go from here and click on Assignment Status to check the history to see whether or not the student has been following the guidelines that were set for the assignment or if the work is just sitting there. It helps the teachers to keep track on who is getting the work done and who may need a little bit of encouragement and can hold some of the students accountable.

This is also a good way for the teacher to determine if they need to provide some extra assistance to their students or not. If they notice that someone has been logging in and doing the work but they are not getting very far, they may be able to come in and see if the student needs a little bit of extra help with the assignment or not. This is a great way to provide some individual help to the student, something that would be almost impossible for the teacher to do in the traditional classroom.

There are so many different things that you will be able to do when you are working with Google Classroom. It has some great features that are perfect for both the student and for the teachers as well, which is why this is one of the top reasons that Google Classroom is one of the best in the industry. Learn how to use the various features that are available with Google

Classroom, and you are going to see some great changes in the way that students learn and teachers teach in no time.

Conclusion

Thank for making it through to the end of *Google Classroom: Student Guide to Google Classroom.* Let's hope it was informative and able to provide you with all of the tools you need to achieve your goals of

The next step is to figure out which class you belong to and start working on Google Classroom. One of the easiest ways for students to start working in Google Classroom is to wait until they get an invitation from their teacher. They can then just click on the link and get all of the account set up. It is possible for students to have more than one classroom set up and organized inside of their account and they can even archive some of their past classes so that they can look for it a little bit later.

There are so many features that both teachers and students are going to be able to enjoy when it comes to using Google Classroom. This is a simple tool that comes with a lot of the great apps that you are used to with Google such as Google Forms, Gmail, Spreadsheets, and so much more. Add in the fact that you are able to sync together the due dates for all of your assignments on Google Calendar so you never have to search for these again, and Google Classroom is quickly going to become your best friend for setting up your classes and keeping everything organized.

This guidebook has spent some time talking about the different things that you are able to do with Google Classroom as a student. So set up your account, try out some of the great features, and see what Google Classroom has to offer to you!

Finally, if you found this book useful in any way, a review on Amazon is always appreciated!

Made in the USA
Columbia, SC
05 November 2017